Perspectives

An Education

A Right or a Privilege?

T0359548

Contents

Introduction

What makes an education more than just learning?

We all have to go to school. We need to learn basic skills such as reading, writing, doing maths and finding out about the world. But is that all education is? Many would say that it is much, much more!

For some people, getting an education can change their lives. Even having one special teacher can influence the direction of your life. And getting an education doesn't always mean sitting in a classroom.

What does an education mean to you? What is important?

4

My views about school

Read these students' opinions about what they like and don't like about school.

What are your views? What do you value most about your education?

Sometimes, my friends complain about school, but I don't. I lived in Afghanistan until my family moved to Australia when I was seven. Not everyone goes to school in Afghanistan – there is a shortage of schools, and if you live too far from your closest school, you just can't go.

And it's worse if you're a girl. There are people in Afghanistan who don't believe girls should go to school at all. And even if they do go, they often leave at a young age because they are forced to marry or to work to help their families. More than half of all girls in Afghanistan don't go to school.

And the schools in Afghanistan are not well equipped like they are here. Sometimes, school is just a tent or a tarpaulin tied to some trees.

That is why I will never take my education for granted.

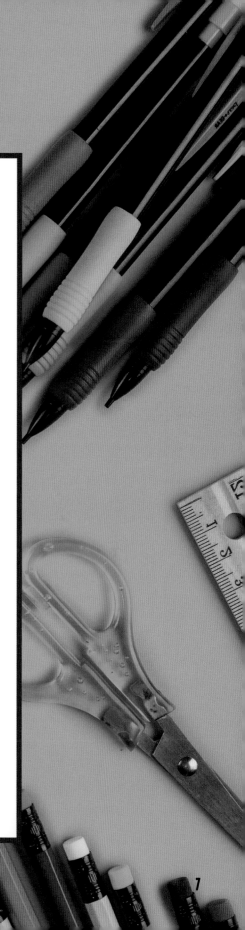

These are my favourite things about school:

- Playing soccer at lunchtime – it's fun and I get to be with my friends.

- Going on excursions – we don't have to do schoolwork, I get to be with my friends and we see interesting things, especially when we go to places like science museums.

- Library time – it's cosy and I like finding books about things I'm interested in.

- In class, I like doing big projects because I get to work with my friends. In Year 4, I had to make a model of a soccer stadium. My mum helped me. Everyone told me that my model was great.

But, I don't like tests. For many students, tests are stressful. This means that these students are not able to perform at their peak ability because they get overwhelmed and find it hard to keep up.

I used to be miserable at school, especially when I first started. I wasn't a good listener, I was always in trouble and I found it hard to learn. It felt like the teachers didn't smile at me the way they smiled at the other kids.

But in Year 3, this changed. My teacher, Miss Hoban, was kind and great at explaining things. Each Monday before school, she helped me with reading. I could tell she liked me and this made a big difference.

I still don't love school, but I'm happy. I have friends, I'm learning lots and I'm confident.

Being homeschooled is sort of complicated. On the one hand, I really like it because I'm always with my dad and we get to do fun activities to learn and my education is tailored completely to me.

For example, I learn by talking – and through conversations, I am able to understand things super quickly. There was one time when I couldn't understand multiplication. So Dad and I baked biscuits, and we doubled the recipe, so I had to multiply all the ingredients.

The only real downside of homeschooling is not getting to see my friends every day, but that doesn't matter too much because I hang out with them on the weekends.

Inspiring educators

Think about all the teachers you have had since you started school. Has one teacher in particular helped you? In what ways did they help you?

Rebecca Katzman asked two successful people about one of their most memorable and inspiring teachers.

Jessica Mauboy

Jessica Mauboy is an award-winning singer, songwriter and actress.

"Music is what feelings sound like and a great music teacher helps you turn your feelings into music," says Jessica.

For Jessica Mauboy, that great music teacher was Judy Weepers.

One day, when Jessica was just seven years old, she was humming to herself in class. Her tuneful humming was distracting her classmates, so her teacher sent her to sit outside the classroom in the corridor.

Music teacher, Judy Weepers, happened to walk by. She heard Jessica singing and invited her to join the school choir. This was the beginning of Jessica's musical education. Judy Weepers continued to give Jessica music lessons as she went on to high school.

"She did it all without payment, all the way through to Year 10. She knew in her heart this was something I loved to do," said Jessica. "When I was 15, she came to support me when I went to Tamworth to compete there and she helped my parents so much to deal with it all … It is amazing to think that without her hearing me humming outside my classroom, none of this would have happened."

Bill Gates

Microsoft cofounder Bill Gates uses his wealth
to help improve health and education worldwide.

I've been lucky to have some amazing teachers. One who stands out for me is Blanche Caffiere, a kind librarian and teacher I first met when I was in Year 4.

I was pretty timid in primary school. I was embarrassed by my lousy handwriting and messy desk, and I tried to hide the fact that I liked to read – something that was cool for girls but not for boys.

Mrs Caffiere helped make it okay for me to be myself. She pulled me out of my shell by sharing her love of reading. She asked me what I was interested in and she found me books – biographies, for example – that were more challenging than the science fiction I was reading at the time. Then she made the time to discuss them with me. She genuinely listened to what I had to say.

Bill Gates watches children use computers he donated at a public library in Washington, DC, USA.

500

BILL & MELI
GATES

I learnt from Mrs Caffiere that my teachers had so much more knowledge to share. I just needed to ask. Mrs Caffiere died in 2006, shortly after her one hundredth birthday. Before she passed, I got to thank her for the role she played in my life. She helped spark my interest in libraries (the first big effort in philanthropy for me and my wife, Melinda) and my belief that every child should get the benefit of great teachers. It's remarkable how much power one good person can have in shaping the life of a child.

Bill Gates (right) and Microsoft cofounder, Paul Allen, at school, 1970

Ready to learn

Angelina Touron loves her job. She is an EAL teacher at a primary school in Melbourne, Australia. (EAL means English as an Additional Language.) She runs a program for children who come from many different countries.

As you read this interview, think about what a difference this program makes for the children who come from different countries. What would help you if you went to a school where the language was different from the one you use?

Q: What is your role at the school?

A: I teach small groups of students who have entered school with little or no English. Some of these students were born overseas and now live in Australia. Others may have been born in Australia, but speak a language other than English in their homes. Some are here as refugees, as the country they were born in experienced war, unrest or other hardship.

All of my students have so much knowledge about the world. They have a lot to offer their peers and teachers. It is my role to help them build confidence as speakers of English, so that they can fully participate in their classroom learning and enjoy the experience of school.

Q. What happens in your program? What do the students do?

A: Many hands-on activities form part of my program, as holding, touching and seeing things help students remember and learn quickly. We play games or do special activities, such as painting, gardening or cooking.

I present the students with language about the topic they are learning in their classrooms, as this helps them learn the vocabulary needed to participate in classroom activities.

Sometimes, the students speak in their first language, as they have so much to say, but do not have the words in English. We read bilingual books together that are written in English and another language. I've learnt new words in other languages, too!

Q: What challenges do your students face?

A: For some students, their experience in an Australian school is quite different from what they had experienced overseas. Working in groups, participating in class discussions and asking questions are all things common to Australian schooling, but not necessarily common to education in all countries.

Some students travelled across several countries before settling in Australia, which took time and disrupted their schooling. These students are working hard to "catch up" on their school work. Another challenge is learning the sounds and writing system of a new language. It is amazing how quickly students meet this challenge.

Q: What feedback have you received from parents?

A: Like all parents, the parents of my students are pleased to see their children happy and learning. They are grateful that their children are thriving. Many parents have expressed how appreciative they are of the education system in Australia.

Q: What do you want people to know about your students?

A: My students are beautiful to teach. They all have positive attitudes. It is inspiring to see them work hard and become more confident in using the English language. I am amazed at how capable they are at making connections between experiences they've had in their first language and what I teach them. My students are generous in sharing aspects about their culture. This helps us all learn together.

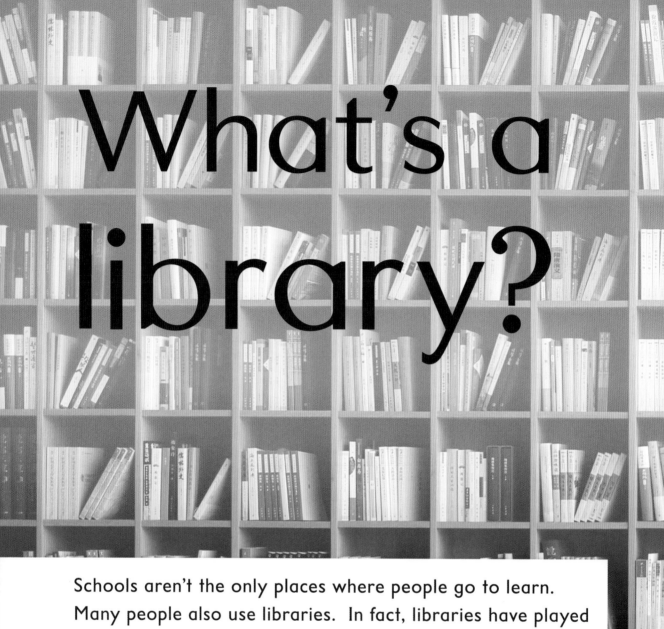

What's a library?

Schools aren't the only places where people go to learn. Many people also use libraries. In fact, libraries have played an important role in educating people for hundreds of years.

In this article, Joshua Hatch examines the role libraries play in our lives today. Do you use a library? What's the most important thing to you about libraries?

You might think a library is a place filled with books where you have to be quiet. Sure, some libraries are like that, but that's not only what a library is.

A library is more like a warehouse of information and knowledge – and even culture. Often, that knowledge is stored as books. But that information can also be stored as CDs or DVDs, audiobooks, e-books, magazines, newspapers, puzzles or even tools.

There are many different kinds of libraries. Your school probably has a library filled with books for students. You can find fiction or nonfiction books there, and reference books like dictionaries and encyclopedias. Some of the books you can borrow and take home. Others, like the reference books, have to stay in the library so others can use them.

Universities, law schools and medical schools have specialised libraries that are filled with materials appropriate for those students. For example, medical schools have scientific medical papers and books about anatomy you won't find in your school library.

"If I was a book, I would like to be a library book, so I would be taken home by all different sorts of kids."
–Cornelia Funke, author

Most cities have public libraries where people can borrow books. Some libraries are in spectacular buildings with grand reading rooms. Others aren't buildings at all, but instead are mobile vehicles that bring books to rural towns.

Once upon a time, libraries were quiet places with signs warning you not to make noise. Now, libraries have spaces set up for exhibitions and performances. They run storytelling sessions for parents of young children. They provide language classes, book clubs and film societies. And there are desks where students can study. And free wi-fi!

When two donkeys arrive with stacks of books, children in Colombia, South America, are happy to see their *biblioburros*!

"When in doubt go to the library."
–Hermione Granger, a character in J. K. Rowling's
Harry Potter and the Philosopher's Stone

This travelling library is a mobile home called a bookmobile.

Some libraries lends tools to gardeners. People borrow rakes, hoes and wheelbarrows. Then there's a public library in Port Macquarie, New South Wales, that goes one step further. It lends *seeds*. Gardeners "borrow" the seeds and plant them. When their plants produce their own seeds, the gardeners are encouraged to save them and donate some back to the library.

Long ago, it was rare for people to own many books. Only wealthy people could afford them. They built private libraries for themselves. But knowledge and information isn't very useful if it's not broadly shared. That's why public libraries are so important. They provide many people with access to knowledge.

Now, a new kind of public library is popping up. People in all kinds of neighbourhoods are erecting small boxes – not much bigger than a microwave – in front of their houses. Called Little Free Libraries, the boxes hold a dozen or so books. People are encouraged to take and donate books. And they don't have to be quiet when they do!

The right to an education

The Universal Declaration of Human Rights is a milestone document in the history of human rights. It was adopted by the United Nations (UN) in 1948.

It set out, for the first time, fundamental human rights to be universally protected. Article 26 of this document details the right to education.

Why did the UN include education in this document?

Article 26

1. Everyone has the right to education. Education shall be free, at least in the elementary and fundamental stages. Elementary education shall be compulsory. Technical and professional education shall be made generally available and higher education shall be equally accessible to all on the basis of merit.

2. Education shall be directed to the full development of the human personality and to the strengthening of respect for human rights and fundamental freedoms. It shall promote understanding, tolerance and friendship among all nations, racial or religious groups, and shall further the activities of the United Nations for the maintenance of peace.

3. Parents have a prior right to choose the kind of education that shall be given to their children.

What is your opinion? How to write a persuasive argument

1. State your opinion

Think about the issues related to your topic. What is your opinion?

2. Research

Research the information you need to support your opinion.

Related *Perspectives* book   Internet   Other sources

3. Make a plan

Introduction

How will you "hook" the reader?

State your opinion.

List reasons to support your opinion.

What persuasive devices will you use?

Reason 1
Support your reason with evidence and details.

Reason 2
Support your reason with evidence and details.

Reason 3
Support your reason with evidence and details.

Conclusion

Restate your opinion. Leave your reader with a strong message.

4. Publish

Publish your persuasive argument.

Use visuals to reinforce your opinion.